Most-Used Shorthand Words and Phrases

CLASSIFIED ACCORDING TO THE LESSONS IN
THE GREGG SHORTHAND MANUAL SIMPLIFIED

John Robert Gregg

Louis A. Leslie

Charles E. Zoubek

GREGG PUBLISHING DIVISION

McGraw-Hill Book Company, Inc.

New York   Chicago   San Francisco   Dallas   Toronto   London

APR --- 2003

MOST-USED SHORTHAND WORDS AND PHRASES

Aug. 1958-RD

Code No. 24542

Shorthand Plates Written by

CHARLES E. ZOUBEK

PUBLISHED BY GREGG PUBLISHING DIVISION

McGraw-Hill Book Company, Inc.

Printed in the United States of America

Printing Statement:

Due to the very old age and scarcity of this book,
many of the pages may be hard to read due to the
blurring of the original text, possible missing pages,
missing text and other issues beyond our control.

Because this is such an important and rare work, we
believe it is best to reproduce this book regardless of
its original condition.

Thank you for your understanding.

PREFACE

Most-Used Shorthand Words and Phrases contains the shorthand outlines for 3,669 words and 1,696 phrases selected on the basis of usefulness and frequency.

The words were selected from the first 10,000 words in order of frequency of the Horn-Peterson *Basic Vocabulary of Business Letters*. That work contains the 14,834 different words found in a count of 1,500,000 words of business letters chosen from 26 kinds of business. The 3,669 words in *Most-Used Shorthand Words and Phrases* were chosen from the first 10,000 in order of frequency on the basis of the greatest usefulness to the stenographer in the business office. Many of the first 10,000 words in order of frequency are simple derivatives in *-ing, -ed, -s* that the shorthand writer can construct for himself when the primitive form is given. In the rare cases when such derivatives present any stenographic problem, they are given. Thus the 3,669 shorthand outlines in the word list comprise almost all the stenographic value of the 10,000 most frequently used words in business dictation. An Index to the words begins on page 113. For each word listed, there is a reference to the lesson in which the word may first be written.

The 1,696 phrases in this book were selected from the 3,536 different phrases found by one of the authors in a business-letter phrase-frequency count of 250,000 running words of business-letter dictation. Approximately one-third of the phrases (1,445) occurred only once in the 250,000 words and therefore do not appear in the present list. It is interesting to note that the first 100 different phrases in order of frequency, with their repetitions, account for 15,631 of the total of 33,202 phrases occurring in the 250,000 running words of dictation.

The key to good phrasing is simplicity. Of the 3,536 different

iii

phrases in the phrase-frequency count, 2,183 contain only two words each.

Chapter I of this book contains 721 words and 326 phrases. Chapter II contains 342 words and 507 phrases. Thus, after completing the first two chapters of the *Gregg Shorthand Manual Simplified,* the learner can write 1,063 of the most useful business words and 833 of the most useful business phrases. The fact that almost exactly half the most useful business phrases may be written after the completion of the first two chapters of the *Manual* emphasizes the simplicity of good phrases.

The shorthand teaching profession owes a great debt to Doctor Horn and to Miss Peterson for their invaluable *Basic Vocabulary of Business Letters.*

The Publishers

CHAPTER I

LESSON 1

A, S-Z, F, V

face		safe		say	
phase		save		vase	

E, N, M

easy		knee		aim	
fee		navy		main	
fees		sane		may	
sea		scene		me	
see		seen		mean	
sees		vain		same	

T, D

ate		stain		deed	
east		stay		feed	
faced		steam		made	
feet		tea		need	
meat		team		saved	
neat		aid		seed	
seat		day		stayed	

1

O, R, L

foe		dear		deal	
know		drain		fail	
no		drove		feel	
note		fair		late	
sew		free		lead	
snow		freight		leave	
so		near		low	
stove		rate		mail	
stow		road		real	
toe		trade		relay	
vote		treat		retail	
zone		wrote		steal	

H

hair		hate		heat	
haste		hear		heed	

Omission of minor vowels

dealer		heater		notary	
Easter		later		phone	
even		meter		reader	
favor		motor		season	
hasten		nearer		total	

LESSON 2

S-Z, P, B

days

hope

able

knows

open

base

least

paid

better

means

paper

blame

niece

pays

boats

notes

people

brief

readers

place

labor

seems

prepare

neighbors

K, G

broke

cream

game

came

keys

gave

claim

sake

girls

clear

taken

grade

close

gain

grow

Sh, Ch, J

shade

chains

age

shaped

cheaper

changed

shares

chose

page

sheep

each

range

show

reached

storage

The diphthong *i*

buy	hide	rise
cried	iron	slight
drive	light	styles
dry	might	tire
dye	night	tried
files	obliged	type
height	rely	vital

LESSON 3

Additional sounds of *a* and dot for *-ing*

add	alarm	aiming
advice	arm	bearing
agree	army	casting
appear	bargain	charming
arrive	charged	evening
average	far	grading
capital	farms	greeting
fast	harm	heating
habit	large	leasing
has	mark	lining
master	star	making
sample	starts	trading

Additional sounds of *e*

bids	bed	church
chickens	check	earn
drill	fellow	firms
familiar	getting	her
given	helped	hurry
him	led	hurt
little	medal	major
middle	pledge	search
river	seller	serve
similar	settle	urge

Upward strokes for *th*

bath	healthy	thickness
birth	lath	thinner
birthday	thick	throat

Phrases

as if	if my	has no
as these	if so	each night
as though	if these	gave me
each case	give me	my dear
each day	has had	so large
has given	has known	so late
has met	has made	so low

Brief forms

a	.	goes	⌐ʒ	its	
ago		going		more	—
am	—	good		not	—
an	.	goods		our	
are		he	°	ours	
at	/	hour		the	
can		hours		well	
cannot		I	O	will	
can't		in	—	wills	
go		it	/	would	

Phrases

are

are not   here are   these are

at

at least   at the   at these

good

as good   good deal

he

he came	he drove	he goes
he can	he fell	he knows
he can make	he felt	he left
he can't	he gets	he lives

he made	he reaches	he will not
he may	he said	he will say
he needs	he will	he would

I

I am	I guess	I reached
I came	I know	I read
I can	I left	I realize
I cannot	I live	I said
I can see	I make	I say
I drove	I mean	I see
I fear	I met	I will
I feel	I might	I will not
I felt	I need	I will see
I gave	I need not	I would
I get	I notice	I would not
I give	I ran	I wrote

in

| in case | in its | in the |
| in it | in our | in these |

it

| as it | if it | it will |
| as it will | it has | it will not |

the

as the		has the	
ask the		if the	

make the

realize the

not

had not   has not   might not

will, well

as well	well known	will pay
so well	will not	will see

LESSON 4

Short sound of *o*

adopt	crossed	logs
block	dock	loss
blotter	dog	lost
bronze	drop	lot
catalogue	hog	mob
clock	hop	model
co-operate	hospital	moderate
copies	hot	mop
copper	job	observe
cottage	jobber	occur
crop	lobby	occurrence
cross	lock	off

offer		pocket		shop	
offset		popular		soft	
often		remodeling		spot	
oftener		rob		stock	
operate		rock		stop	
opposite		rod		top	

Aw

abroad		brought		jaw	
absorb		caught		laws	
auto		cause		ought	
bought		caused		raw	
broad		clause		saw	
broadcasting		daughter		talked	
broader		draw		taught	

Phrases

across the		he saw		I talked	
has taught		he talked		I thought	
he lost		I saw		off the	

Brief forms

be		by		have	
before		could		herewith	
but		for		his	

is	)	ship	/	therefore	
of	υ	their	/	therein	
put	(	there	/	which	/
shall	/	thereby		with	

Phrases

be

can be		I will be		might not be	
cannot be		I would be		need be	
can't be		if it will be		need not be	
he can be		in behalf		on behalf	
he will be		it will be		she may be	
he would be		it will not be		will be	
I can be		may be		will not be	
I cannot be		may not be		would be	
I can't be		might be		would not be	

by

| by it | | by mail | | by these | |
| by its | | by the | | by which | |

could

could be		he could		I could be	
could not		he could not		I could not	
could not be		I could		I could see	

for

for his		for my		for these	
for it		for our		for which	
for its		for the		for which the	
for me		for their		before the	

have

can have		I have		I would have	
have given		I have had		it will have	
have had		I have made		may have	
have made		I have not		might have	
have not		I have tried		will have	
he will have		I may have		will not have	
he would have		I will have		would have	

is, his

as it is		if it is		is there	
he is		in his		it is	
he is not		is it		on his	
he is the		is not		she is	
here is		is the		she is not	

of

of his		of our		of their	
of it		of ours		of these	
of its		of the		of which	

shall

I shall	I shall make	shall be
I shall be	I shall not	shall not
I shall have	I shall see	shall not be

there, their

as there	if there will	there may be
as there is	there are	there will
if there are	there is	there will be
if there is	there may	there would be

with

with him	with the	with which
with our	with these	with which the

which

in which	on which the	which may
in which the	which is	which may be
on which	which is the	which means

LESSON 5

The combination *ses*

access	analysis	balances
addresses	arises	bases
advances	assessed	basis
advices	auspices	braces

cases		glasses		premises	
causes		leases		presses	
census		lenses		prices	
chances		losses		releases	
classes		mattresses		says	
clauses		necessitate		services	
closes		necessity		sister	
courses		notices		sizes	
criticism		nurses		sources	
faces		passes		spaces	
finances		places		versus	

To in phrases

as to be		to break		to fill	
has to be		to burn		to finance	
is to be		to buy		to finish	
to balance		to change		to fit	
to be		to charge		to fly	
to bear		to check		to follow	
to beat		to face		to have	
to bite		to fall		to jar	
to blame		to farm		to park	
to borrow		to feel		to pass	

to pay	to see	to spare
to pick	to sell	to speed
to place	to separate	to spread
to plan	to serve	to supply
to play	to serve you	to surprise
to post	to share	to survey
to prepare	to shift	to visit
to preserve	to ship	to which
to put	to show	to which the
to say	to slide	to which you

Strokes for *x*

affix	fixes	taxed
box	flax	taxes
boxed	mix	taxicab
boxes	mixed	text
fix	mixer	textile
fixed	tax	

LESSON 6

Circles inside curves
Two curves in the same direction

appeal	bear	built
barrel	belt	buyer

| cave | | give | | park | |
| gift | | pair | | spare | |

At the beginning or end of curves

apply		error		happy	
again		gay		heavy	
arm		gray		help	
art		half		if	
cry		happen		pay	

Straight line and curve joining without angle

accurate		dig		light	
bread		flat		read	
bright		gauge		rid	
cash		hosiery		plate	
cashier		jar		share	
catch		jelly		shell	
chair		journal		sharp	
charge		kitchen		take	

Outside angles
Between straight lines

chain		match		net	
jam		met		omit	
machine		metal		teacher	

Straight line and curve joining with angle

arrange	finish	mile
bad	fit	milk
battery	fresh	mill
benefit	get	oblige
bid	green	pin
branch	guide	plain
bridge	hotel	plan
campaign	ledger	ran
cheap	line	reach
chief	make	shape
clean	map	telephone
dark	March	tell
decline	margin	territory
deep	marked	tip
federal	material	tire
final	merit	type

Between two curves

back	clearer	factory
bag	clerk	farm
baggage	clipping	fell
beg	draft	file
cabinet	driver	fill

firm		liberty		pig	
fur		library		prefer	
label		life		prepare	
labor		live		private	
larger		package		rapid	
learn		paper		traffic	
left		people		travel	
liberal		pick		trip	

Circles on straight lines

adding		die		mighty	
adhere		edges		mine	
admit		enamel		my	
aging		had		pretty	
ample		head		ready	
army		height		remedy	
attached		hit		she	
chairman		imagine		tie	
data		lady		tied	
dictate		man		title	

Between two reverse curves

black		car		cargo	
break		care		carload	

carry	gallon	legal
cracked	gear	paragraph
drag	guilty	rag
fabric	kill	regret
fiber	lack	telegraph
flag	leg	track

O hook on its side

Before *n*

alone	known	stone
drawn	loan	thereon
grown	on	thrown
honor	owner	tone

Before *m*

home	homes	omit

Before *r*

abnormal	floor	narrower
cordial	horn	nor
corn	horses	normal
corner	ignore	or
course	lower	oral
door	moral	orange
drawer	mortgage	organ

origin	storm	tore
original	story	torn
store	torch	

Before *l*

call	golf	recall
coal	hole	roller
collar	holiday	small
college	knowledge	whole
dollar	pay roll	wholesale

Phrases

he calls	on its	on the
I call	on our	on these
on it	on sale	or more

Downward character preceding *o*

ball	fault	salt
baseball	follow	shown
bolt	foreign	solicit
bone	pole	solid
born	policy	solve
borrow	polish	sorrow
borrowers	politics	source
fall	porch	vault

Clockwise *th*

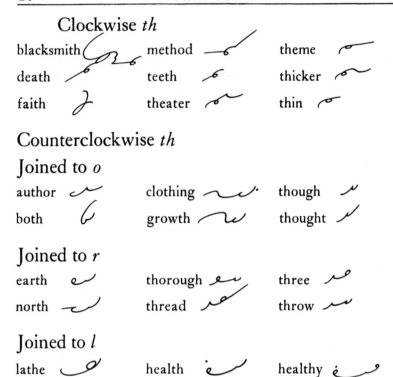

blacksmith   method   theme

death   teeth   thicker

faith   theater   thin

Counterclockwise *th*

Joined to *o*

author   clothing   though

both   growth   thought

Joined to *r*

earth   thorough   three

north   thread   throw

Joined to *l*

lathe   health   healthy

CHAPTER II

LESSON 7

Brief forms

Dear Sir		must		write	
Dear Sirs		right		year	
desire		rights		years	
desires		that		you	
hereto		them		your	
market		to		yours	
Mr.		were		Yours truly	

Phrases

must

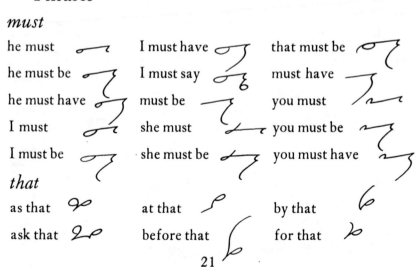

he must	I must have	that must be
he must be	I must say	must have
he must have	must be	you must
I must	she must	you must be
I must be	she must be	you must have

that

as that	at that	by that
ask that	before that	for that

21

hope that	that are	that may be
hope that the	that are not	that our
hoping that	that have	that the
if that is	that is	that their
in that	that is not	that there are
is that	that is the	that there is
is that the	that it	that these
of that	that it has	that will
on that	that it is	that will be
on that day	that its	that will not
realize that	that it will	that would
so that	that it will be	that would be
so that the	that may	with that

them

ask them	in them	to them
for them	of them	with them

to

as to	to care	to claim
as to that	to carry	to clean
as to the	to cash	to clear
to call	to catch	to climb
to cancel	to cause	to close

to gain	to its	to their
to get	to taste	to these
to give	to take	to tie
to go	to talk	to trade
to grow	to tell	to train
to his	to that	to travel
to it	to the	to try

you

as you	asking you	if you care
as you are	before you	if you could
as you can	by you	if you get
as you go	can you	if you go
as you have	for you	if you have
as you know	have you	if you have not
as you may	hope you will	if you know
as you may have	give you	if you need
as you say	giving you	if you see
as you will	if you	if you will
as you will see	if you are	if you will be
as you would	if you are not	if you will have
as you would be	if you can	if you will see
ask you	if you can be	if you will ship
asking me	if you cannot	if you would

if you would be	you cannot see	you might
if you would have	you can see	you might be
in which you	you can't	you might have
in which you are	you could	you might not
of you	you could be	you need
reach you	you could have	you need not
serving you	you could not	you say
to have you	you could see	you see
to which you are	you have	you shall have
to you	you have had	you will
which you	you have made	you will be
which you can	you have not	you will have
which you may	you have seen	you will not
with you	you know	you will not be
you are	you made	you will not have
you are not	you make	you will see
you can	you may	you would
you can be	you may be	you would be
you can have	you may have	you would have
you cannot	you may not	you would not

your

as to your		for your		on your	
as your		have your		to your	
ask your		if your		with your	
before your		of your		your name	
by your		of yours		your needs	

were

if it were		there were		were not

write

I write		I will write		write me

Miscellaneous

for Mr.		I desire		My dear sir
he desires		if you desire		you desire

Word beginning *ex-*

example	expedite	explains
exceed	expense	express
exceeding	expenses	expressed
except	expensive	exterior
excess	expert	extra
excessive	expire	extras
exchange	expires	extreme
exhibit	explain	inexpensive

LESSON 8

Word endings *-tion, -tial, -cient, -ciency*

-tion, -cient, -ciency

action	exemption	portion
ancient	exhibition	possession
application	expansion	precaution
authorization	expiration	preparation
cancellation	expression	prescription
caution	fashion	prevention
collision	illustration	protection
co-operation	mission	ration
collection	motion	relation
corporation	national	section
declaration	occasion	sectional
efficient	operation	selection
efficiency	option	session
election	patient	taxation
exception	physician	vacation

-tial

beneficial	financial	partial
essential	initial	social
essentials	official	special

Phrases

for collection ⟋ in relation ⟋

Past tense, -er, -or

initialed ⟋	marketed ⟋	writer ⟋
desired ⟋	shipped ⟋	writers ⟋

LESSON 9

Brief forms

been ⟋	pleased ⟋	then ⟋
from ⟋	pleasing ⟋.	they ⟋
like ⟋	should ⟋	was ⟋
please ⟋	than ⟋	when ⟋

Phrases

from

from its ⟋	from his ⟋	from that ⟋
from these ⟋	from it ⟋	from them ⟋
hear from you ⟋	from our ⟋	from you ⟋
from him ⟋	from the ⟋	from which ⟋

like

he liked ⟋	I should not like ⟋	would like ⟋
I like ⟋	if you like ⟋	you liked ⟋
I should like ⟋	if you would like ⟋	you would like ⟋

please

please be	please ship	please write me
please have	please sign	to please
please see	please write	

should

he should	I should have	should not be
he should be	I should say	you should
he should have	should be	you should be
I should	should have	you should have
I should be	should like	you should not

than, then

less than	less than the	since then
less than that	more than	than the

they

as they	that they	they can't
as they are	that they are	they could
before they	that they will	they could not
if they	they are	they have
if they are	they are not	they may
if they are not	they can	they may be
if they can	they can be	they must
if they would	they can have	they will
if they would be	they cannot	they will be

they will have   they will see   they would buy

they will not   they would   they would not

when

when our   when the   when they

when that   when these   when they are

was

he was   that it was   was that

I was   that there was   was the

it was   there was   which was

it was the   was it

Been in phrases

could have been   have not been   there has been

had been   having been   there have been

Able in phrases

be able   he will be able   shall be able

been able   he will not be able   to be able

Word endings -*ly*, -*ily*, -*ally*

-*ly*

amply   clearly   earlier

badly   closely   early

barely   daily   excessively

briefly   deeply   extremely

fairly	likely	rapidly
favorably	only	rarely
firmly	mainly	separately
freely	merely	simply
highly	namely	sincerely
inevitably	nearly	slightly
largely	nicely	slowly
lately	possibly	thoroughly

-ily, -ally

cordially	finally	nationally
easily	financially	normally
especially	heartily	occasionally
essentially	heavily	originally
exceptionally	legally	principally
families	locally	readily
family	materially	totally

LESSON 10

The diphthong *oi*

annoyance	boy	coin
annoyed	boys	hoist
avoid	choice	join
boiler	coil	joy

loyal   poison   toy

noise   royal   voice

oil   soil   void

Word endings -*ure*, -*ture*

failure   lecture   pasture

feature   literature   picture

Word endings -*ual*, -*tual*

actual   equal   schedules

actually   equally   semiannual

Omission of vowel in word beginnings

re-

reason   region   resale

reasonably   register   research

be-

became   begin   below

because   beginning   behalf

began   begins   betray

de-

debit   deliberate   depot

delays   deposits   derive

des-, dis-

describe   description   despite

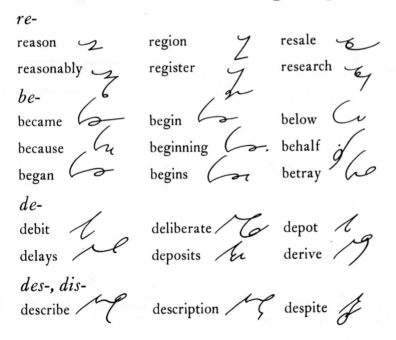

destroy	discrepancy	dismissal
disbursed	discretion	dispatch
disclose	disease	display
discouraged	dismiss	dissolved

mis-

miscarry	misleading	mistake
mislaid	misplaced	mistaken

Phrases

he received	I received	to feature
I described	in response	to figure
I disliked	to begin	to join

LESSON 11

Brief forms

after	business	hand
all	businesses	handed
and	businesslike	most
aside	decide	mostly
besides	decided	Mrs.
billing	decidedly	sides
bills	end	what

Phrases

after

after that　*{shorthand}*　　after them　*{shorthand}*　　after which　*{shorthand}*

after the　*{shorthand}*

and

and are　*{shorthand}*	and see　*{shorthand}*	and they　*{shorthand}*
and have　*{shorthand}*	and that　*{shorthand}*	and was　*{shorthand}*
and his　*{shorthand}*	and that is　*{shorthand}*	and which　*{shorthand}*
and is　*{shorthand}*	and the　*{shorthand}*	and will　*{shorthand}*
and our　*{shorthand}*	and their　*{shorthand}*	and will be　*{shorthand}*
and say　*{shorthand}*	and these　*{shorthand}*	and will not　*{shorthand}*

side

he decided　*{shorthand}*　　I decided　*{shorthand}*　　if you decide　*{shorthand}*

what

what are　*{shorthand}*	what is　*{shorthand}*	what will　*{shorthand}*
what has been　*{shorthand}*	what is the　*{shorthand}*	what will be　*{shorthand}*

Miscellaneous

all right　*{shorthand}*　　　　for most　*{shorthand}*　　of all　*{shorthand}*

Any vowel after the diphthong *i*

appliance　*{shorthand}*	diameter　*{shorthand}*	science　*{shorthand}*
bias　*{shorthand}*	diet　*{shorthand}*	trial　*{shorthand}*
diagnosis　*{shorthand}*	drier　*{shorthand}*	via　*{shorthand}*
dial　*{shorthand}*	prior　*{shorthand}*	violation　*{shorthand}*

The dotted circle

appreciate		bacteria		obviate	
appreciation		beneficiary		piano	
area		create		radiation	
areas		depreciation		radiator	
association		librarian		variation	

Hook and circle vowels joined

drawee		poetry		radio	
poems		poets		snowy	

LESSON 12

Been in phrases

had not been		I have been		which have been
has been		it has been		would have been
has not been		should have been		you have been
have been		to have been		you have not been

Able in phrases

being able		he should be able		will be able
has been able		he would be able		you may be able
has not been able		I have not been able		you must be able
have been able		I shall be able		you should be able
have not been able		I shall not be able		you will be able
he may be able		I will be able		you would be able

Word beginning *re-*

reappear	refining	reserved
reasons	repair	resources
rebate	repeat	response
receipt	replace	reveal
receive	replied	reverse
reception	reservation	revise
rechecked	reserve	revision

E written in *re-*

reclaim	regain	rename
recline	remake	retake

Word beginning *de-*

decision	deposit	deserve
delay	depositor	design
delayed	depository	designer

E written in *de-*

decay	declare	decline

CHAPTER III

LESSON 13

The *oo* hook

ŭ

above	drug	shovels
apparatus	duck	status
blood	dug	stub
bud	dust	stuff
bulbs	illustrate	suction
bulk	illustrations	suffer
butter	luck	sufficient
chorus	oven	thus
color	plug	tough
couple	plus	truck
cup	production	trust
cups	reduction	tub
cut	reproduction	uneven
disastrous	rough	up
discussion	rub	upper
does	rubber	utterly

36

ŏŏ

book	foot	looked
booked	full	pull
bushel	fully	push
cook	hook	stood
cooker	look	sugar
		took

ōō

accrued	grew	route
blue	group	routine
booth	grouped	rule
boots	jewel	school
bouquet	jewelers	screw
cool	jewelry	shoe
coupon	juvenile	spoon
crude	loose	through
do	lose	tool
drew	pool	tooth
exclude	poor	tour
exclusive	prune	true
food	roof	who
fruit	room	whom
glued	root	withdrew

Phrases

do, does

do it	if you do	you do not like
do not	if you do not	does not
do not have	if you do not like	does not have
do so	that do not	he does
do you	they do	he does not
I do	they do not	that does not
I do not	you do	this does not
I do not like	you do not	which does

who, whom

who are	who knows	who should
who can	who like	who should be
who can be	who made	who takes
who cannot	who make	who taught
who could	who makes	who will
who desire	who may	who will be
who do not	who may be	who would
who go	who might	who would be
who have	who might be	who would have
who have had	who might have.	who would like
who have made	who might like	who would not
who is	who must	to whom

Miscellaneous

above the	I took	to choose
check up	I trust	to cut
for whom	through its	to fuss
he discussed	through that	to push
he looks	through the	to shoot
he took	through them	to trust
I discussed	through these	up to
I look	to book	up to the

Words beginning w, sw, wh

wa

highway	waiver	wear
wages	waste	wears
wagon	wave	weigh
waist	way	weighed
wait	ways	weight

wi

wide	wire	wise
wife	wires	wives

we

we	width	worries
west	win	worse
wet	witness	worst

wo

walk ⟋	warm ⟋	water ⟋
wall ⟋	wash ⟋	woe ⟋
walnut ⟋	washer ⟋	worn ⟋
war ⟋	watch ⟋	woven ⟋

woo

wool ⟋	woolen ⟋	wood ⟋

sw

swam ⟋	sweet ⟋	swivel ⟋
swear ⟋	swell ⟋	sworn ⟋
sweater ⟋	switch ⟋	swollen ⟋

wh

whale ⟋	wheel ⟋	whip ⟋
wheat ⟋	while ⟋	white ⟋

Phrases

as we	if we do	we can have
as we are	if we have	we can make
as we have	we are	we cannot
if we	we are not	we cannot be
if we can	we are sure	we can say
if we can be	we call	we can't
if we cannot	we can	we could
if we could	we can be	we could be

we could have	we have not had	we shall not
we could not	we know	we shall not be able
we decide	we made	we shall see
we decided	we make	we should
we desire	we may	we should be
we do	we may be	we should have
we do not	we may be able	we should like
we do not say	we may have	we should not like
we do not see	we mean	we should say
we feel	we might	we take
we feel sure	we might be able	we took
we get	we must	we tried
we give	we must have	we trust
we have	we need	we try
we have been	we note	we will
we have been able	we notice	we will be
we have decided	we shall	we will have
we have given	we shall be	we will not
we have had	we shall be able	we will not be
we have made	we shall have	we will see
we have not	we shall mail	we will ship
we have not been	we shall make	we would
we have not been able	we shall need	we would be

we would have	𝓏	we would not	𝓎	which we	⌁
we would like	𝓏	we would not be able	𝓎	which we are	⌁

LESSON 14

Brief forms

about	⌒	gladly	⌒	thing	⌒
booklet	⌒	let	⌒	think	⌒
enclose	⌒	letter	⌒	this	⌒
enclosed	⌒	letters	⌒	very	⌒
enclosure	⌒	nothing	⌒	worth	⌒
glad	⌒	send	⌒	worthy	⌒

Phrases

about

about it	⌒	about that	⌒	about these	⌒
about its	⌒	about the	⌒	about this	⌒
about my	⌒	about them	⌒	about which	⌒
				about your	⌒

this

after this	⌒	do this	⌒	if this is	⌒
as this	⌒	for this	⌒	if this is not	⌒
at this	⌒	from this	⌒	if this is the	⌒
before this	⌒	hope that this	⌒	in this	⌒
by this	⌒	if this	⌒	in this case	⌒

in this way   this is   this was the

of this   this is not   this will

on this   this is the   this would

on this side   this man   this would be

since this   this may   to this

that this   this may be   up to this

that this is   this means   when this

this can be   this was   with this

let, letter

and let   I have your letter   please let

as your letter   if you let   this letter

do not let   in that letter   we have your letter

for your letter   let me   your letter

thing, think

as you think   I think   to think

if you think   if they think   we do not think

do you think   same thing   who think

I do not think   they think   you think

glad

be glad   I shall be glad   we shall be glad

he will be glad   I should be glad   we would be glad

he would be glad   shall be glad   will be glad

I am glad   they will be glad

send

please send	send this	sending the
send him	send us	sending them
send them	send you	sending us
		sending you

very

very glad	very good	very well

enclose

I enclose	we enclose	you enclosed

Word ending -*ther*

another	father	mother
bother	feather	neither
bothered	gather	rather
brother	other	together
either	others	weather
farther	leather	whether

Phrases

each other	other side	to gather
he gathered	other than	whether or not
I gathered	to bother	

LESSON 15

The sound of *w* in the body of a word

Broadway	quick	roadway
dwelling	quicker	railway
equip	quiet	requisition
equipped	quit	reservoir
liquid	quite	square
queen	quota	twice
query	quote	twin

Phrases

to quit	to quote	we quoted

Ah, aw

ahead	awaiting	aware
await	awake	away

The sound of *y*

yacht	yeast	yes
yarn	yell	yoke
yarns	yellow	youth

LESSON 16

Brief forms

belief	believer	delivered
believe	deliver	deliveries

doctor	return	satisfied
during	returned	satisfy
necessarily	satisfaction	work
necessary	satisfactorily	worked
next	satisfactory	yet

Phrases

as necessary	I believe	next meeting
as yet	I do not believe	next year
has not yet	I returned	next year's
has not yet been	if necessary	of work
have not yet	in return	please return
he returns	is not yet	to believe

Omission of short ŭ

Before n

begun	lunch	runs
bunch	luncheon	son
done	punch	sun
gun	run	ton
fun	runner	tonnage

Before m

become	column	drum
bumper	come	lumber

lump ⌒⁊   some ⌒   summary ⌒⌒

plumbing ⌒⌒   something ⌒⌒   summer ⌒⌒

pump ⌒⁊   sum ⌒   welcome ⌒⌒

Before a downstroke

brush ⌐⁊   crushed ⌒⁄   rush ⌒⁊

brushed ⌐⁊   flush ⌐⁊   rushed ⌒⁄

budget ⌐   judge ⁄   rushing ⌒⁊.

clutch ⌒⁊   much ⁄⌐⁊   touch ⁄

Phrases

as much ⁊⌐   I have done ⁊⌐   to be done ⁄⌐

be done ⁄⌐   I come ⌒⌒   to become ⌐⌒

being done ⌐⁄   much more ⌐⌐   to come ⌒⌒

can be done ⁊⌐   much more than ⌐⌐   to judge ⁄

cannot be done ⌒⁊   must be done ⌐⌐   too much ⁄⌒⌐

can't be done ⌒⁊   please rush ⌒⌐⁊   very much ⌐⁊⁊

could be done ⌒⁄⁄   should be done ⁄⁄   we have done ⁄

has come ⁊⌐   so much ⁊⁊   who comes ⌒⌒⁊;

has done ⁊⁄   something like ⌒⌒   who have done ⁄

have done ⁄   they come ⌒⌒   will be done ⌒⁄⌐

                         would be done ⁄⁄

Strokes for *ng* and *ngk*

ng

angle	ring	string
bring	shingle	strong
hanger	sing	strongly
hung	single	swing
king	song	tongue
language	spring	wrong
length	strength	young

ngk

anchor	crank	link
ankle	drinking	pink
bank	frank	sanction
banker	frankly	shrinkage
bankruptcy	functions	sink
banquet	handkerchief	tank
blank	ink	trunk
blanket	junction	uncle

LESSON 17

Brief forms

accompanied	among	bookkeeping
along	belong	companies

company	over	thank
great	overcharge	under
greater	overlooked	undercharges
greatly	oversight	undersized
keep	oversize	understood
kept	remit	where
long	remittance	whereabouts
longer	remittances	whereas
nowhere	remitted	wherein

Phrases

along the	thank you for this
along this	thank you for your
among the	thank you for your letter
among them	this company
among these	to keep
as long	to thank you for
if you keep	to thank you for your
so long	we thank you for
thank you	we thank you for the
thank you for	we thank you for your
thank you for the	

Strokes for *rd* and *ld*

rd

accordance	favored	preferred
answered	garden	prepared
appeared	guard	record
assured	harder	registered
award	hard	repaired
awarded	hardly	retired
bird	hardware	seaboard
board	hazard	stored
border	heard	suffered
burden	hired	third
card	ignored	tired
colored	occurred	toward
cord	offered	word
corduroy	orchard	wired
expired	pardon	yard

ld

billed	canceled	failed
boiled	child	field
build	children	filed
builders	cold	filled
called	drilled	fold

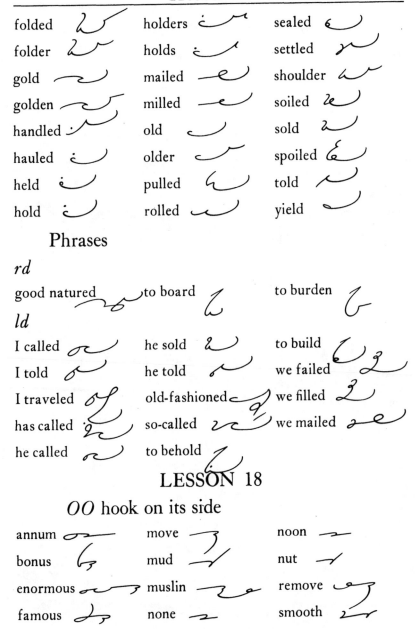

folded	holders	sealed
folder	holds	settled
gold	mailed	shoulder
golden	milled	soiled
handled	old	sold
hauled	older	spoiled
held	pulled	told
hold	rolled	yield

Phrases

rd

| good natured | to board | to burden |

ld

I called	he sold	to build
I told	he told	we failed
I traveled	old-fashioned	we filled
has called	so-called	we mailed
he called	to behold	

LESSON 18

OO hook on its side

annum	move	noon
bonus	mud	nut
enormous	muslin	remove
famous	none	smooth

Word endings *-ure, -ual*

-ure

fixtures	natural	secure
mature	naturally	signature
moisture	pictures	structure
nature	procure	structural

-ual

annual	gradual	scheduling
annually	gradually	virtually

After a downstroke

assurance	measure	surely
assure	measures	treasurer
assures	pleasure	treasury
juries	pressure	casually
jury	sure	visual

Phrases

sure

be sure	feeling sure	to be sure
being sure	I am sure	you can be sure
can be sure	if you are sure	you may be sure
feel sure	please be sure	

The combination *us*

adjust	choose	justly
adjusts	desirous	nervous
ambitious	discuss	religious
anxious	discussed	shoes
anxiously	just	us
bus	justice	whose

Phrases

before us	gave us	on us
by us	give us	to give us
for us	giving us	with us
from us	hear from us	

Comma *s* with *f, v, k, g;* left *s* with *p, b, r, l*

accept	busy	decrease
address	basket	drastic
answer	cancel	elastic
apiece	capacity	errors
applies	case	facilitate
arisen	cast	fails
arrives	checks	fast
ask	cigars	favors
backs	class	feels
bags	clerks	fiscal

gas	pencil	service
gasoline	piece	shelves
girls	pigs	sketch
gives	pipes	space
glass	raise	specific
graphs	realize	speed
grocery	release	separate
guess	risk	spirit
helps	ropes	spoke
lamps	sacrifice	spread
lease	safety	supplied
least	salary	surprise
less	sales	tags
list	salesman	teachers
listen	scheme	tracer
lives	score	trips
makes	scrap	vast
maps	search	vicinity
marks	secretary	visit
parcel	sells	wholesale
pass	series	

Comma s before t, d, n, m, o; left s after those characters

absence	fellows	miss
advance	finance	names
agencies	firms	needs
arms	frames	notice
astray	frozen	pins
assets	glance	plans
balance	grades	post
bids	gross	practice
chance	happens	principal
chosen	hats	rates
Christmas	heads	rose
city	homes	sad
claims	illness	said
close	knows	sample
coast	ladies	seats
courtesy	lessons	sedan
currency	lines	seems
days	machines	semester
desk	magazine	sense
establishing	means	set
farms	medicine	shades

sheets	smoke	statistics
shows	snap	step
sickness	soap	still
sign	solicit	story
similar	source	style
simple	staff	task
since	stamp	tickets
sincere	start	vacancies

Comma *s* before and after *sh, ch, j*

branches	dishes	packages
bridges	ditches	pages
changes	edges	reaches
charges	hinges	sash
cheese	matches	siege
chest	messages	wrenches

Words consisting of *s* or *s* and *th* and a circle vowel

| as | say | seethe |
| has | see | these |

CHAPTER IV

LESSON 19

The diphthong *u*

acute	fewer	tube
argue	fuel	unique
bureau	peculiar	unite
cubic	pure	unit
cure	review	utilization
dispute	reviews	view
few	tribune	views

The diphthong *ow*

aloud	flowers	power
blouse	loud	proud
bow	mouth	south
cow	now	southeast
crowd	ounce	towels
doubt	plow	tower
flour	powder	voucher

Phrases

in view	I doubt	right now
few days	in our power	we doubt

57

Brief forms

ever		one		use	
every		out		used	
how		outline		whatever	
importance		outside		whenever	
important		soon		wherever	
matters		sooner		without	
once		those		won	

Phrases

about those		for one		one-half	
along those		for one thing		one way	
among those		for those		one year	
and those		from those		only one	
as those		how much		that those	
at those		in this matter		this matter	
by those		in those		this one	
each one		of those		to those	
ever since		one thing		very important	
every one		on this matter		when those	
every other		once more		with those	

LESSON 20

Brief forms

always	suggest	weak
any	suggested	week
anyone	suggestion	weekly
anything	unable	wish
gone	unusually	wished
several	usual	world

Phrases

always be	for any one	if anything
any more	for any other	if you wish
any one	for anything	of any
any other	has gone	one week
any others	have gone	several days
business world	I wish	several other
for any	if any	several others

Blended consonants *ted, ded, det*

ted

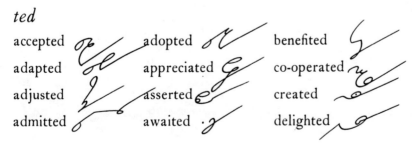

accepted	adopted	benefited
adapted	appreciated	co-operated
adjusted	asserted	created
admitted	awaited	delighted

depleted	listed	solicited
deposited	noted	started
doubted	omitted	steadily
executed	operated	steady
excited	pasted	studied
exhibited	posted	studies
fitted	quoted	study
hesitated	rated	today
homestead	related	treated
illustrated	repeated	united
lifted	repeatedly	visited
limited	routed	waited
liquidated	separated	wasted

ded

added	deductions	headed
dead	graded	loaded
deduction	guided	needed

det, dit

audit	credits	detailed
auditor	debt	ditto
credit	debtor	editor
credited	detail	editorial

Phrases

he needed   I needed   I noted

Blended consonants *m-n*, *m-m*

administer	manner	minimum
aluminum	manual	minute
cement	many	money
eliminate	maximum	month
examine	meant	monthly
examiner	member	nominal
examined	memo	prominence
freshmen	memorial	remain
harmony	memory	remained
human	men	romance
immensely	mental	salesmen
lemon	mention	summons
manage	mentioned	tremendous
manager	mineral	woman
managers	miniature	women

Phrases

as many	few minutes	I doubted
each month	few months	I mention
every minute	he mentioned	I mentioned
every month	how many	I remain

in this manner	next month	this month
in this month's	several months	to mention
many other	so many	we mention
many others	these men	you mentioned

LESSON 21

Blended consonants *nt*, *nd*

nt

absent	current	parents
acquainted	disappoint	plant
apparent	eccentric	planted
applicant	event	pleasant
appointed	eventually	plenty
aunt	excellent	point
bent	front	prevent
brilliant	grant	prevented
cent	granted	printer
center	guarantee	prominent
central	hints	recent
centralized	hunting	rent
century	joint	rental
client	jointly	rented
country	paint	sent

silent   venture   went

talent   warrant   winter

vacant   warranted   won't

nd

assigned   designed   outlined

band   fastened   owned

behind   find   phoned

beyond   friend   planned

bind   fund   refund

binder   gained   render

bindery   grand   rendered

blunder   grind   sand

bond   island   sandals

bonded   joined   second

brand   kind   secondary

burned   kindness   signed

calendar   land   splendid

candy   lands   surrender

canned   learned   surrendered

cleaned   lend   trained

cylinder   lined   trend

earned   loaned   unearned

explained   overburdened   wind

Phrases

aren't	I sent	we don't
as you will find	if we don't	we find
doesn't	if you don't	we shouldn't
don't	isn't	we wouldn't
hadn't	isn't it	weren't
hasn't	shouldn't	who doesn't
haven't	they don't	who isn't
he couldn't	to bind	will find
he finds	to find	wouldn't
he isn't	to paint	you aren't
I couldn't	to plant	you couldn't
I don't	to point	you don't
I find	to prevent	you haven't
I haven't	to print	you will find
I learned	we couldn't	you wouldn't

Blended consonants *mt, md*

ashamed	framed	prompt
claimed	fumed	promptly
deemed	gummed	promptness
exempt	jammed	seemed
famed	named	trimmed

Initial vowel omitted

anticipate	endorse	entry
anticipated	endorsed	index
anticipation	endorser	indexes
antique	entire	industry
emptied	entirely	intelligence
empty	entitled	into

Phrases

into it	into the	into these
into that	into them	into this

Brief forms

big	did	office
bigger	general	offices
bigness	generally	officers
date	got	opportunity
dated	individual	want
dates	morning	wanted

Phrases

as you did	he didn't	I got
did not	he got	if you did not
didn't	I did	if you didn't
he did	I did not	next morning
he did not	I didn't	office manager

on that date	we did	who didn't
they did	we did not	you did
this date	we didn't	you did not
this morning	we got	you didn't

LESSON 22

Omission of vowels
Circle omitted from *u*

absolute	manufacture	produced
avenue	manufactured	producers
due	manufacturer	produces
dues	manuscript	reduce
duly	music	reduced
duty	mutual	reduces
enumerated	mutually	renew
induce	new	renewal
issue	newer	renewed
issued	news	revenue
issues	numerous	suit
knew	overdue	suited
lieu	produce	volume

Other vowel omissions

auditorium	millions	serious
courteous	miscellaneous	seriously
erroneous	period	situated
genuine	premium	theory
graduate	previous	union
graduation	previously	vacuum
ideal	radius	various

Phrases

he knew	in lieu	we knew
I knew	to produce	you knew

Days and months

Sunday	January	July
Monday	February	August
Tuesday	March	September
Wednesday	April	October
Thursday	May	November
Friday	June	December
Saturday		

Phrases

Friday morning	Tuesday morning
Friday night	Wednesday morning
Saturday morning	Thursday morning

LESSON 23

Omission of *ow*

around	count	down
account	counted	found
accountant	counter	foundry
accounted	counting	ground
background	county	round
brown	crown	sound
council	discount	surrounding
counsel	discounted	town

moun

amount	amounting	mount
amounted	amounts	mounted

jog

announce	announced	announces

Phrases

he found	to count	we found
I found	we count	

Word beginnings *per-, pro-, pur-*

per-

per	percentage	perhaps
per cent	perforated	permanent

permit	person	personnel
permitted	personal	persuade
perpetual	personally	persuaded
perplexing	persons	persuasion

pro-

approach	proceed	proof
approached	process	proper
appropriate	processes	properly
appropriation	professional	proportion
approval	professor	proportionate
approve	profit	proprietor
approved	profitably	prosperous
approximate	prohibit	prove
apron	promise	proved
fireproofing	promised	proven
probate	promises	provide
problem	promote	provided
procedure	promotion	provision

pur-

| purloin | pursuant | pursued |
| purple | pursue | pursuit |

Phrases

it will prove	to permit	to promote
per hour	to persuade	to prove
per month	to proceed	to provide

-ment

adjustment	endorsement	monument
agreement	equipment	movement
allotment	establishment	nonpayment
announcement	experiment	ornamental
appointment	experimental	payment
arrangement	fundamental	replacement
assessment	garment	settlement
assignment	inducement	shipment
basement	judgment	supplement
casement	management	supplemental
document	measurement	supplementary
elementary	moment	treatment
elements	momentary	

Phrases

few moments	in payment

-ble

acceptable	adjustable	agreeable
adaptable	advisable	applicable

appreciable	favorable	reasonable
available	feasible	reliable
cable	flexible	responsible
capable	inadvisable	salable
desirable	liable	suitable
double	payable	table
eligible	possible	trouble
equitable	profitable	unaccountable

CHAPTER V

LESSON 25

-ship

fellowship	membership	scholarship
hardship	ownership	steamship
kinship	relationship	township

-cle, -cal

analytical	mechanical	practical
article	mechanically	practically
chemical	medical	radical
chemicals	musical	statistical
critical	periodical	surgical
geographical	periodically	technical
historical	physical	typical
logical	political	typographical

-self, -selves

herself	myself	themselves
himself	oneself	yourself
itself	ourselves	yourselves

72

Phrases

for itself   *⟋*   for themselves *⟋⟋*   in itself *⟋*

for myself *⟋*   for yourself *⟋*   of ourselves *⟋*

for ourselves *⟋*   for yourselves *⟋*   with themselves *⟋*

After-

aftermath *2⟋*   afternoon *2*   afterthought *2⟋*

LESSON 26

Brief forms

enable   progressive   speaks

order   property   street

ordered   purpose   streets

orders   purposes   such

progress   speak   upon

Phrases

in order   on such   upon this

in order that   to speak   upon us

in such   upon such   upon which

no such   upon the   upon you

of such   upon them   with such

Blended consonants *pent, pend, gent*

pent, pend

appendix   carpenter   depend

dependable	expended	respondent
depended	expenditure	spend
dependent	happened	spent
depends	opened	suspend
expend	pending	

gent

cogent	gentle	intelligently
diligently	gentleman	urgent
genteel	intelligent	urgently

Blended consonants *def, dev, tive*

def

defense	devised	difference
defer	develop	different
deferred	developed	diversion
defiance	development	divert
definite	develops	diverted
defy	devote	divide
device	devoted	divided
devise	differ	division

tive

appreciative	co-operative	descriptive
authoritative	creative	executive

initiative	native	positively
locomotive	negative	relative
motive	positive	scientific

Phrases

| to spend | to defeat | to devote |

LESSON 27

Electr-, electric

electric	electrician	electronics
electrical	electricity	electros
electrically	electric wire	electrotype

Inter-

interfere	intermediate	interrupted
interference	internal	interruption
interim	international	interval
interior	interpreted	interview

intr-

| introduce | introduced | introduction |

enter-

enter	entering	entrance
entered	enterprise	entrances

Short-

| short | shortages | shorter |
| shortage | shorten | shortly |

ship-

| shipwreck | shipshape | shipmate |

LESSON 28

Words modified in phrases

as soon as

| as soon as | as soon as possible | as soon as the |

hope

I hope	I hope to see	we hope these
I hope that	we hope	we hope this
I hope that the	we hope that	we hope to have
I hope the	we hope that these	we hope you can
I hope these	we hope that this	we hope you will
I hope this	we hope the	

I had

| I had | I had been | I had not |

us

| let us | let us know | please let us |
| let us have | let us say | to us |

to

to do	to do the	to himself
to do it	to do this	to our
to do so	to him	to ourselves

order

if your order   thank you for your order   your order

of your order   you ordered   your orders

Miscellaneous

of course   of course it is   worth while

Use of blend for *not*

he wasn't	it is not	that it was not
I was not	it isn't	there isn't
if it isn't	it was not	this was not
if it was not	it wasn't	was not
if there is not	that it is not	wasn't

Ago in phrases

centuries ago	months ago	some years ago
few days ago	several days ago	weeks ago
few months ago	several months ago	years ago
long ago	some weeks ago	

Want in phrases

he wanted	I want	if you want
he wants	I wanted	they want

we want	who want	you want
we wanted	who wanted	you wanted

LESSON 29
Word endings -ful, -ify

-ful

awful	doubtful	hopeful
beautiful	faithful	powerful
careful	grateful	thoughtful
carefully	helpful	useful
delightful	helpfulness	usefulness

-ify

amplifier	diversified	notify
amplify	gratified	ratify
beautify	gratifying	specified
certified	justified	specify
certify	justify	testify
classified	modify	verify

Phrases

to beautify	to specify	to verify

-ification

classification	modification	ratification
edification	notification	specifications
justification	qualifications	verification

-gram

cablegram	monogram	telegram
diagram	program	telegrams

-rity

authorities	majority	securities
charity	maturity	security
clarity	prosperity	surety

-lity

ability	inability	possibilities
advisability	liabilities	qualities
disability	locality	reliability
facilities	nobility	responsibility
facility	personality	sensibilities

-lty

casualty	loyalty	royalty
faculty	penalty	

CHAPTER VI

LESSON 31

Blended consonants *ten, den*

ten

acceptance	extensively	stenographer
attend	extent	stenographic
attended	gotten	straighten
attention	hesitancy	straightened
bulletin	itinerary	tenant
button	maintenance	tend
carton	patent	tender
cotton	retention	tendered
destined	rotten	tent
distance	satin	tentative
extension	sentence	tonight
extensive	standard	written

den

abandon	audience	dinner
accident	danger	evidence
attendance	deny	evident

80

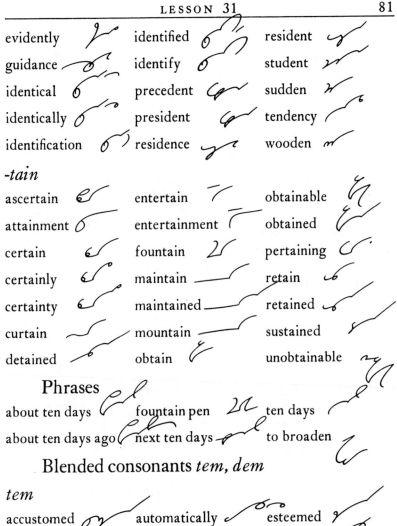

evidently   identified   resident

guidance   identify   student

identical   precedent   sudden

identically   president   tendency

identification   residence   wooden

-tain

ascertain   entertain   obtainable

attainment   entertainment   obtained

certain   fountain   pertaining

certainly   maintain   retain

certainty   maintained   retained

curtain   mountain   sustained

detained   obtain   unobtainable

Phrases

about ten days   fountain pen   ten days

about ten days ago   next ten days   to broaden

Blended consonants *tem, dem*

tem

accustomed   automatically   esteemed

attempt   bottom   estimate

attempted   custom   estimated

attempting   customary   item

automatic   customer   itemized

legitimate	temperature	timber
stomach	temple	tomatoes
system	temporarily	tomorrow
temper	temporary	

dem

damage	dimensions	medium
damaged	domestic	random
demonstrate	freedom	redemption
demonstration	kingdom	seldom

Special business forms

to know	Sincerely yours
to make	Very cordially yours
to me	Very respectfully yours
Cordially yours	Very sincerely
Dear Madam	Very sincerely yours
Dear Miss	Very truly
Dear Mrs.	Very truly yours
Dear Mr.	Yours cordially
Gentlemen	Yours respectfully
My dear Miss	Yours sincerely
My dear Mr.	Yours very respectfully
My dear Mrs.	Yours very sincerely
Respectfully yours	Yours very truly

LESSON 32

Brief forms

difficult	outstanding	standing
difficulty	purchase	standpoint
extraordinary	purchased	stands
meantime	purchases	time
merchandise	purchasing	times
merchant	sometime	understand
ordinarily	sometimes	understandable
ordinary	stand	why

Phrases

about that time	by the time	on time
about the time	by this time	one time
about this time	each time	several times
after that time	few times	since that time
any time	for the time	some time
at all times	from time	some time ago
at that time	in time	such time
at the time	long time	that time
at this time	many times	this time
at which time	next time	to purchase
before that time	of that time	to time
by that time	of time	why not

Tern, term; dern, derm; thern, therm

attorney	modern	termed
determine	northern	terminal
determined	northwestern	terminate
eastern	pattern	terms
eternal	southeastern	thermometer
external	southern	turn
fraternity	southwestern	turned
lantern	term	western

Phrases

he turned	I turned	to turn

Syllable *ort*

assorted	port	report
assortment	portable	reported
court	portfolio	reports
deportment	ports	resort
export	quart	sort
headquarters	quarter	sport
mortal	quarterly	sports

LESSON 33

-ct

abstract	effect	productive
act	effective	project
acted	elect	prospect
active	exact	prospective
actively	exactly	protect
activity	expect	protected
acts	expected	reflect
affect	expects	reflected
affected	fact	rejected
affects	facts	respect
attractive	inactive	respectfully
collect	intact	respectively
collected	neglected	select
deduct	perfect	selected
deducted	perfectly	strictly
defect	predict	tract
district	product	tractor

Phrases

affect the	fact that this	to perfect
fact that	in fact	to protect
fact that the	to collect	to select

One-syllable words ending in *st*

best	last	rested
cost	lasting	resting
costing	lasts	rests
costly	past	test
costs	past-due	tested
first	rest	tests

Phrases

at last	in the last	last time
first time	last minute	last year
for the last	last month	last year's
for the past	last night	past year

-*st*

against	earnestly	honestly
artist	exhaust	honesty
assist	exhausted	interest
assistance	exist	interested
assistant	existed	interesting
attested	existence	interests
cheapest	exists	kindest
chemistry	finest	largest
closest	harvest	latest
earnest	honest	nearest

protest *Cl*   quickest *⌀⟋*   resistance *⥿*

protested *Cl,*   resist *⌐*   slightest *⥿ol*

Phrases

against the *⟋⌐*   to protest *Cl*   against your *⟋⥿*

Disjoined word endings *-ist, -est*

earliest *⌀⟋*   highest *⟋*   prettiest *Co⟋*

easiest *⟋*   lowest *⌐⟋*   shortest *⟋*

greatest *⌐⟋*   newest *⌐⟋*   slowest *⌐⟋*

LESSON 34

Brief forms

advertise *⟋*   else *⌐⟋*   presented *C,*

advertisement *⟋⌐*   elsewhere *⌐⟋*   probable *⟋*

body *⟋*   part *⟋*   probably *⟋*

consider *⌐⟋*   participate *⟋*   remember *⌐⟋*

considerably *⌐⟋*   parties *⟋⟋*   represent *⌐*

consideration *⌐⟋*   party *⟋*   representative *⌐*

considered *⌐⟋*   presence *C*   represented *⟋⌐,*

departing *⟋.*   present *C*   represents *⌐*

Phrases

anyone else *⌐⟋*   he considers *⌐⟋*   into consideration *⟋⌐*

anything else *⌐⟋*   I consider *⌐⟋*   nothing else *⌐⟋*

at present *⌐*   I remember *⌐⟋*   on our part *⌐⟋*

he considered *⌐⟋*   if you consider *⟋⌐*

remember that	to part	we shall consider
something else	to present	which we consider
to consider	we consider	you will remember

Omission of *d*

amend	diamond	pound
amended	dividend	pounds
amendment	extend	recommend
bound	extended	recommended
bundles	extends	remind
demand	mind	reminded

LESSON 35

Incl-

inclement	include	included
inclined	includes	inclusive

Post-

postage	posthaste	postpaid
postal	postmark	postpone
post card	postmaster	postponed
postdate	post office	postscript

Super-, supr-

superb	supervision	supports
superficially	supervisor	supremacy
superior	support	supreme

Trans-

transact	transit	transmittal
transaction	transition	transmitted
transfer	translated	transparent
transferred	translation	transcribe
transfers	transmit	transcript

CHAPTER VII

LESSON 37

Con-

concealed	confess	consign
concentrate	confidential	consigned
conception	confine	consignee
concern	confined	consignment
concerned	confirm	consist
concerns	confirmed	consisted
concert	conflict	consistent
concession	congested	consistently
concrete	congestion	consists
condense	conjunction	consolidate
condensed	connected	constant
conduct	connection	constantly
conducted	connections	construct
conductor	conscientious	constructed
confer	consent	construction
conference	conservative	constructive

contact	continue	convention
contain	continued	conversation
contained	continues	conversion
container	continuous	convert
contemplate	contract	converted
contemplated	contracted	convey
content	contractor	convince
contention	contracts	discontinue
contest	contrary	discontinued
continent	contrast	reconcile
contingent	control	reconstruction
continuance	controversy	

com-

accommodate	commitments	companion
accomplish	committed	comparative
accomplished	committee	compare
combine	commodities	compared
command	commodity	comparison
commence	common	compel
commend	commonly	compelled
comment	communities	compensation
commerce	community	compete
commercial	compact	competent

competitive
competitor
competitors
compiled
complaint
complete

completed
completely
completion
compliance
compliment
complimentary

comply
compound
comprehensive
compressor
comedian
comedies

Phrases

to compare
to complain
to complete
to comply

to conceal
to confide
to confirm
to conserve

to consist
to continue
to convince
we continue

En-

encountered
encourage
encouraged
encouragement
encroachment
endeavor
engage

engaged
engagement
engine
engineer
engineers
engrave
engraver

enjoy
enjoyed
enlarge
enrolled
en route
enthusiastic
enthusiasm

in-

incapable
incentive
inch

incident
incidental
incidentally

income
incorporated
increase

increased	inside	intend
increases	insist	intended
incurred	insisted	intends
indebted	inspection	intention
indebtedness	inspiration	intimate
indeed	install	intimated
indemnity	installation	invariably
infants	installed	inventory
infer	installment	invest
inferior	instead	invested
inferred	instruct	investment
influence	instructed	invite
injured	instruction	invited
injuries	instructor	invoice
injury	instructive	invoiced
inlaid	instrument	invoices
insert	insurance	involved
inserted	insure	superintendent
insertion	insured	

un-

uncertain	undoubtedly	unfilled
unclaimed	unduly	unjust
undecided	unfair	unloaded

unpacked   unreasonable   unsettled

unpaid   unsatisfactory   until

unn-

unknown   unnecessary   unnoticed

Phrases

we invite   you intend   who intend

we insist   we intend   your intention

Em-

embarrass   emphasis   employed

embarrassment   emphatically   employees

embraces   empire   employment

im-

impairment   impossible   imprinting

impartial   impracticable   improper

imperative   impress   improved

implements   impressed   improvement

import   impression   reimburse

imported   imprint   reimbursed

imports   imprinted   reimbursement

imm-

immodest   immoral   immortal

LESSON 38

For-, fore-

afford	forerunner	forth
effort	forget	fortune
efforts	form	fourth
force	formal	inform
forced	former	informed
foreclosure	formerly	misfortune
foreman	forms	unfortunate

fur-

furlough	furnish	furniture
furnace	furnished	further
furnaces	furnishing	furthermore

Phrases

inform us	setting forth	to forfeit
inform you	to force	to form
informing us	to forego	to furnish
set forth	to forget	to perform

Al-

almost	alter	alternatives
already	alterations	although
also	alternate	altogether

Sub-

subchief	submit	subscription
subdivision	submitted	substance
subeditor	subordinate	substantial
subhead	subscribe	substantiate
sublet	subscriber	subtracted
		subway

Ul-

adult	culminate	resulted
agriculture	culture	resulting
consult	multiple	results
consulted	result	ultimate

-ward

afterward	backward	onward
awkward	forward	reward
awkwardly	forwarded	upward

-hood

boyhood	hardihood	neighborhood
childhood	manhood	parenthood

Phrases

I submit	to consult	to forward

LESSON 39

Abbreviating principle

-use

accuse	confusing	inexcusable
accusation	confusion	refusal
confuse	excuse	refused
confused	excuses	refuses

-titude

aptitude	fortitude	latitude
attitude	gratitude	multitude

-cate

adequate	duplicate	indicates
advocate	duplicated	locate
certificate	inadequate	located
communicate	indicate	reciprocate
confiscate	indicated	syndicate

-cation

allocation	duplication	eradication
communication	education	indication
confiscation	educational	location

-gate

aggregate	corrugated	investigate

-gation

investigation   irrigation   obligation

Phrases

I refuse   to confuse

LESSON 40
Abbreviating principle (continued)

-quire

acquire   inquire   require

acquirement   inquiries   required

esquire   inquiry   requirements

-ntic

Atlantic   authentic   frantic

-ology

apology   biology   psychological

apologies   physiology   technology

apologize   psychology   terminology

-tribute

attribute   contribution   distribution

contribute   distribute   distributors

contributed   distributed   retribution

-quent

consequently   eloquent   frequently

delinquent   frequent   subsequent

-itis

appendicitis *Cb*   tonsillitis *(~P*   neuritis *~P*

-iety

variety *Lo*   society *y*   propriety *Ce*

-titute, -titution

constitute *~76*   institution *~7o/*   substitute *Yo*

institute *~7o*   restitution *~7o/*   substitution *Yo/*

LESSON 41

Abbreviating principle (concluded)

algebra	curriculum	memorandums
alphabet	inconvenience	philosophy
alphabetical	inconvenienced	preliminary
arithmetic	inconvenient	privilege
convenience	equivalent	privileges
convenient	memoranda	privileged
conveniently	memorandum	reluctant

-tition, -tation, -dition, -dation, -nition, -nation,
-mition, -mation

accommodation	combination	competition
addition	commendation	condition
additional	commission	confirmation
admission	commissioner	consolidation

consultation   imitation   recommendation

destination   information   repetition

discrimination   interpretation   reputation

donation   invitation   solicitation

edition   notation   station

estimation   omission   stationed

examination   permission   stationery

explanation   petition   suspension

foundation   quotation   transmission

hesitation   recitation   transportation

Phrases

any information   in addition   to petition

CHAPTER VIII

LESSON 43

Words omitted in phrases

able to work		glad to say	
as a result		glad to see	
at a loss		I should like to have	
at a time		I should like to know	
at such a time		in a few days	
bill of sale		in a few months	
by the way		in addition to the	
during the last		in addition to this	
during the past		in order to be	
for a few days		in order to become	
for a few minutes		in relation to the	
for a long time		in such a manner	
for a minute		in the market	
for a moment		in the past	
glad to have		in the world	
glad to know		line of business	

line of goods		out of the	
line of work		out of them	
many of the		out of this	
many of them		out of town	
men and women		should like to have	
more and more		should like to see	
more or less		some of our	
none of the		some of the	
none of them		some of them	
on the market		some of these	
one of our		some of this	
one of the		some of those	
one of the best		son-in-law	
one of the most		such a thing	
one of them		two or three	
one of these		up and down	
one of those		up to date	
one or two		we should like to have	
ought to have		week or two	
out of date		will you please	
out of that			

Understand, understood

actually understand	my understanding
better understand	please understand
better understanding	readily understand
easily understand	to understand
friendly understanding	we cannot understand
has understood	we hope you will understand
I could understand	we understand
I do not understand	we understand that
I understand	with the understanding
it is understood	you can understand
misunderstanding	you do not understand
misunderstood	you will understand
mutual understanding	

LESSON 44

Compound words

anybody	everything	notwithstanding
anyhow	everywhere	somebody
anything	hereafter	someone
anywhere	heretofore	somewhere
everybody	however	Thanksgiving
everyone	nobody	whatsoever

| whensoever | whomsoever | within |
| wheresoever | whosoever | withstand |

LESSON 45

Brief forms

acknowledge	publication	regular
acknowledged	publications	regularly
acknowledgment	publish	situation
estate	published	state
future	publishers	stated
never	quantities	statement
public	quantity	states

Phrases

| in the future | in this state | to publish |

Phrases

| per gallon | per hundredweight | per pound |

LESSON 46

Brief forms

allow	corrected	envelopes
allowance	correction	experience
allowed	correctly	experienced
correct	envelope	experiences

idea 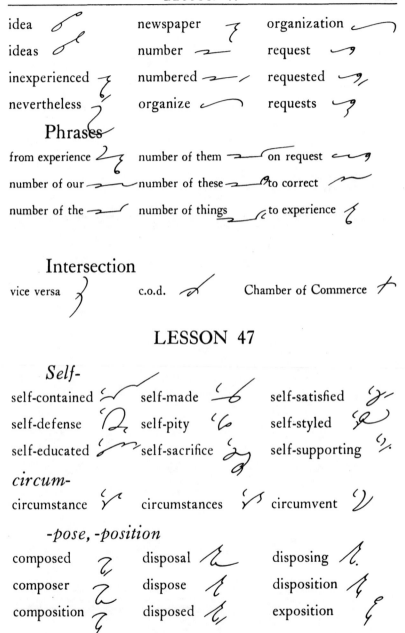 newspaper organization

ideas number request

inexperienced numbered requested

nevertheless organize requests

Phrases

from experience number of them on request

number of our number of these to correct

number of the number of things to experience

Intersection

vice versa c.o.d. Chamber of Commerce

LESSON 47

Self-

self-contained self-made self-satisfied

self-defense self-pity self-styled

self-educated self-sacrifice self-supporting

circum-

circumstance circumstances circumvent

-pose, -position

composed disposal disposing

composer dispose disposition

composition disposed exposition

imposed	proposed	suppose
opposed	proposes	supposed
position	proposition	supposition
proposal	propositions	transposition

Phrases

| in a position | I suppose | to suppose |

Compound word beginnings

| unenterprising | uncompromising | uncontrollable |
| disinclination | incomprehensible | uninsured |

CHAPTER IX

LESSON 49

Brief forms

agent	discovered	regard
agents	immediate	regards
between	immediately	throughout
cover	opinion	valuation
covered	question	value
covers	questions	valued

Phrases

between the	I am of the opinion	throughout the
between these	in our opinion	throughout this
between this	in question	to cover
between us	in regard	to value
between your	out of the question	we are of the opinion
		with regard

-ings

bearings	buildings	clippings
beginnings	casings	earnings

107

drawings	holdings	pleadings
evenings	linings	proceedings
feelings	offerings	savings
fittings	meetings	servings
furnishings	openings	things
hearings	paintings	

-ingly

accordingly	increasingly	seemingly
exceedingly	approvingly	unknowingly

Phrases

in this morning's	so many things	such things
many things	Friday mornings	this morning's

LESSON 50

Brief forms

conclude	house	particularly
concluded	household	particulars
conclusion	houses	subject
conclusive	object	success
confidence	objection	successes
confident	particular	warehouse

Phrases

in particular	on the subject	in conclusion

-sume, -sumption

assume *2*	consume *2*	presume *4*
assumed *2*	consumed *2*	presumed *4*
assumes *2*	consumer *2*	presumptive *4*
assuming *2*	consuming *2*	resume *2*
assumption *2*	presumably *4*	resumed *2*

-ulate

accumulate *oo*	circulating *6*	speculation *4*
accumulated *oo*	circulation *6*	stimulate *γ*
accumulation *oo*	congratulate *2*	stimulated *γ*
calculate *2*	congratulations *2*	stimulates *γ*
circulated *6*	population *ζ*	tabulation *ℓ*

Phrases

I presume *4*	I presume that *4*	to calculate *2*

LESSON 51

Brief forms

advantage *9*	directed *∕*	railroad *⌣*
advantages *9*	direction *∕*	railroads *⌣*
correspond *⌐*	directly *∕*	recognize *⌐*
correspondence *⌐*	director *∕*	recognized *⌐*
corresponding *⌐*	directors *∕*	refer *γ*
direct *∕*	enough *7*	reference *γ*

referred	refers	wondering
referring	wonder	yesterday

Phrases

good enough	to which you refer	with reference
I wonder	we directed	with reference to the

-less

doubtless	hopeless	unless
helpless	needless	worthless
uselessly	helplessness	heartless

LESSON 52

Brief forms

automobile	etc.	likewise
character	govern	otherwise
characters	government	prosecute
circle	instance	prosecution
circular	instant	remainder

Phrases

for instance	to govern	in this instance
		to prosecute

Geographical terminations

-burg

Pittsburgh   Newburgh   Fitchburg

Harrisonburg   Plattsburg   Greensburg

-ville

Jacksonville   Evansville   Brownsville

Gainesville   Louisville   Coatesville

Knoxville   Nashville   Zanesville

-field

Winfield   Pittsfield   Bloomfield

Mansfield   Springfield   Plainfield

-port

Bridgeport   Newport   Gulfport

Westport   Logansport   Glassport

LESSON 53

Geographical terminations

-ford

Stamford *[shorthand]*   Bedford *[shorthand]*   Medford *[shorthand]*

Rockford *[shorthand]*   Hartford *[shorthand]*   Bradford *[shorthand]*

-ington

Torrington *[shorthand]*   Washington *[shorthand]*   Lexington *[shorthand]*

Bloomington *[shorthand]*   Burlington *[shorthand]*   Arlington *[shorthand]*

Huntington *[shorthand]*   Irvington *[shorthand]*   Wilmington *[shorthand]*

-ingham

Framingham *[shorthand]*   Cunningham *[shorthand]*   Buckingham *[shorthand]*

-ton

Evanston *[shorthand]*   Princeton *[shorthand]*   Cranston *[shorthand]*

-town

Morristown *[shorthand]*   Norristown *[shorthand]*   Tarrytown *[shorthand]*

Allentown *[shorthand]*   Lewistown *[shorthand]*   Jamestown *[shorthand]*

Phrases

New York, New York *[shorthand]*   Buffalo, New York *[shorthand]*

Chicago, Illinois *[shorthand]*   San Francisco, California *[shorthand]*

St. Louis, Missouri *[shorthand]*   Boston, Massachusetts *[shorthand]*

Rochester, New York *[shorthand]*

INDEX TO WORDS

(Note: *a, 3* means that the word may first be written in Lesson 3, in *Gregg Short-hand Simplified.*)

114

115

cut, 13
cylinder, 21
daily, 9
damage, 31
damaged, 31
danger, 31
dark, 6
data, 6
date, 21
dated, 21
dates, 21
daughter, 4
day, 1
days, 2
dead, 20
deal, 1
dealer, 1
dear, 1
Dear Sir, 7
Dear Sirs, 7
death, 6
debit, 10
debt, 20
debtor, 20
decay, 12
December, 22
decide, 11
decided, 11
decidedly, 11
decision, 12
declaration, 8
declare, 12
decline, 6
decrease, 18
deduct, 33
deducted, 33
deduction, 20
deductions, 20
deed, 1
deemed, 21
deep, 6
deeply, 9
defect, 33
defense, 26
defer, 26
deferred, 26
defiance, 26
definite, 26
defy, 26
delay, 12
dalayed, 12
delays, 10
deliberate, 10
delighted, 20
delightful, 29
delinquent, 40
deliver, 16
delivered, 16
deliveries, 16
demand, 34
demonstrate, 31
demonstration, 31
deny, 31
departing, 34
depend, 26
dependable, 26
depended, 26
dependent, 26
depends, 26
depleted, 20
deportment, 32
deposit, 12
deposited, 20
depositor, 12
depository, 12
deposits, 10
depot, 10
depreciation, 11
derive, 10
describe, 10

description, 10
descriptive, 26
deserve, 12
design, 12
designed, 21
designer, 12
desirable, 23
desire, 7
desired, 8
desires, 7
desirous, 18
desk, 18
despite, 10
destination, 41
destined, 31
destroy, 10
detail, 20
detailed, 20
detained, 31
determine, 32
determined, 32
develop, 26
developed, 26
development, 26
develops, 26
device, 26
devise, 26
devised, 26
devote, 26
devoted, 26
diagnosis, 11
diagram, 29
dial, 11
diameter, 11
diamond, 34
dictate, 6
did, 21
die, 6
diet, 11
differ, 26
difference, 26
different, 26
difficult, 32
difficulty, 32
dig, 6
diligently, 26
dimensions, 31
dinner, 31
direct, 51
directed, 51
direction, 51
directly, 51
director, 51
directors, 51
disability, 29
disappoint, 21
disastrous, 13
disbursed, 10
disclose, 10
discontinue, 37
discontinued, 37
discount, 23
discounted, 23
discouraged, 10
discovered, 49
discrepancy, 10
discretion, 10
discrimination, 41
discuss, 18
discussed, 18
discussion, 13
disease, 10
dishes, 18
disinclination, 47
dismiss, 10
dismissal, 10
dispatch, 10
display, 10
disposal, 47
dispose, 47

disposed, 47
disposing, 47
disposition, 47
dispute, 19
dissolved, 10
distance, 31
distribute, 40
distributed, 40
distribution, 40
distributors, 40
district, 33
ditches, 18
ditto, 20
diversified, 29
diversion, 26
divert, 6
diverted, 26
divide, 26
divided, 26
dividend, 34
division, 26
do, 13
dock, 4
doctor, 16
document, 23
does, 13
dog, 4
dollar, 6
domestic, 31
donation, 41
done, 16
door, 6
double, 23
doubt, 19
doubted, 20
doubtful, 29
doubtless, 51
down, 23
draft, 6
drag, 6
drain, 1
drastic, 18
draw, 4
drawee, 11
drawer, 6
drawings, 49
drawn, 6
drew, 13
drier, 11
drill, 3
drilled, 17
drinking, 16
drive, 2
driver, 6
drop, 4
drove, 1
drug, 13
drum, 16
dry, 2
duck, 13
due, 22
dues, 22
dug, 13
duly, 22
duplicate, 39
duplicated, 39
duplication, 39
during, 16
dust, 13
duty, 22
dwelling, 15
dye, 2
each, 2
earlier, 9
earliest, 33
early, 9
earn, 3
earned, 21
earnest, 33
earnestly, 33

earnings, 49
earth, 6
easiest, 33
easily, 9
east, 1
Easter, 1
eastern, 32
easy, 1
eccentric, 21
edges, 6
edification, 29
edition, 41
editor, 20
editorial, 20
education, 39
educational, 39
effect, 33
effective, 33
efficiency, 8
efficient, 8
effort, 38
efforts, 38
either, 14
elastic, 18
elect, 33
election, 8
electric, 27
electric wire, 27
electrical, 27
electrically, 27
electrician, 27
electricity, 27
electronics, 27
electros, 27
electrotype, 27
elementary, 23
elements, 23
eligible, 23
eliminate, 20
eloquent, 40
else, 34
elsewhere, 34
embarrass, 37
embarrassment, 37
embraces, 37
emphasis, 37
emphatically, 37
empire, 37
employed, 37
employees, 37
employment, 37
emptied, 21
empty, 21
enable, 26
enamel, 6
enclose, 14
enclosed, 14
enclosure, 14
encountered, 37
encourage, 37
encouraged, 37
encouragement, 37
encroachment, 37
end, 11
endeavor, 37
endorse, 21
endorsed, 21
endorsement, 23
endorser, 21
engage, 37
engaged, 37
engagement, 37
engine, 37
engineer, 37
engineers, 37
engrave, 37
engraver, 37
enjoy, 37
enjoyed, 37
enlarge, 37
enormous, 18
enough, 51

116

117

genuine, 22
geographical, 25
get, 6
getting, 3
gift, 6
girls, 2
give, 6
given, 3
gives, 18
glad, 14
gladly, 14
glance, 18
glass, 18
glasses, 5
Glassport, 52
glued, 13
go, 3
goes, 3
going, 3
gold, 17
golden, 17
golf, 6
gone, 20
good, 3
goods, 3
got, 21
gotten, 31
govern, 52
government, 52
grade, 2
graded, 20
grades, 18
grading, 3
gradual, 18
gradually, 18
graduate, 22
graduation, 22
grand, 21
grant, 21
granted, 21
graphs, 18
grateful, 29
gratified, 29
gratifying, 29
gratitude, 39
gray, 6
great, 17
greater, 17
greatest, 33
greatly, 17
green, 6
Greensburg, 52
greeting, 3
grew, 13
grind, 21
grocery, 18
gross, 18
ground, 23
group, 13
grouped, 13
grow, 2
grown, 6
growth, 6
guarantee, 21
guard, 17
guess, 18
guidance, 31
guide, 6
guided, 20
guilty, 6
Gulfport, 52
gummed, 21
gun, 16
habit, 3
had, 6
hair, 1
half, 6
hand, 11
handed, 11
handkerchief, 16
handled, 17
hanger, 16

happen, 6
happened, 26
happens, 18
happy, 6
hard, 17
harder, 17
hardihood, 38
hardly, 17
hardship, 25
hardware, 17
harm, 3
harmony, 20
Harrisonburg, 52
Hartford, 53
harvest, 33
has, 3
haste, 1
hasten, 1
hate, 1
hats, 18
hauled, 17
have, 4
hazard, 17
he, 3
head, 6
headed, 20
headquarters, 32
heads, 18
health, 6
healthy, 3
hear, 1
heard, 17
hearings, 49
heartily, 9
heartless, 51
heat, 1
heater, 1
heating, 3
heavily, 9
heavy, 6
heed, 1,
height, 2
held, 17
help, 6
helped, 3
helpful, 29
helpfulness, 29
helpless, 51
helplessness, 51
helps, 18
her, 3
hereafter, 44
hereto, 7
heretofore, 44
herewith, 4
herself, 25
hesitancy, 31
hesitation, 41
hide, 2
highest, 33
highly, 9
highway, 13
him, 3
himself, 25
hinges, 18
hints, 21
hired, 17
his, 4
historical, 25
hit, 6
hog, 4
hoist, 10
hold, 17
holders, 17
holdings, 49
holds, 17
hole, 6
holiday, 6
home, 6
homes, 6
homes, 18
homestead, 20

honest, 33
honestly, 33
honesty, 33
honor, 6
hook, 13
hop, 4
hope, 2
hopeful, 29
hopeless, 51
horn, 6
horses, 6
hosiery, 6
hospital, 4
hot, 4
hotel, 6
hour, 3
hours, 3
house, 50
household, 50
houses, 50
hesitated, 20
how, 19
however, 44
human, 20
hung, 16
hunting, 21
Huntington, 53
hurry, 3
hurt, 3
I, 3
idea, 46
ideal, 22
ideas, 46
identical, 31
identically, 31
identification, 31
identified, 31
identify, 31
if, 6
ignore, 6
ignored, 17
illness, 18
illustrate, 13
illustrated, 20
illustration, 8
illustrations, 13
imagine, 6
imitation, 41
immediate, 49
immediately, 49
immensely, 20
immodest, 37
immoral, 37
immortal, 37
impairment, 37
impartial, 37
imperative, 37
implements, 37
import, 37
importance, 19
important, 19
imported, 37
imports, 37
imposed, 47
impossible, 37
impracticable, 37
impress, 37
impressed, 37
impression, 37
imprint, 37
imprinted, 37
imprinting, 37
improper, 37
improved, 37
improvement, 37
in, 3
inability, 29
inactive, 33
inadequate, 39
inadvisable, 23
incapable, 37
incentive, 37

inch, 37
incident, 37
incidental, 37
incidentally, 37
inclement, 35
inclined, 35
include, 35
included, 35
includes, 35
inclusive, 35
income, 37
incomprehensible, 47
inconvenience, 41
inconvenienced, 41
inconvenient, 41
incorporated, 37
increase, 37
increased, 37
increases, 37
increasingly, 49
incurred, 37
indebted, 37
indebtedness, 37
indeed, 37
indemnity, 37
index, 21
indexes, 21
indicate, 39
indicated, 39
indicates, 39
indication, 39
individual, 21
induce, 22
inducement, 23
industry, 21
inevitably, 9
inexcusable, 39
inexpensive, 7
inexperienced, 46
infants, 37
infer, 37
inferior, 37
inferred, 37
influence, 37
inform, 38
information, 41
informed, 38
initial, 8
initialed, 8
initiative, 26
injured, 37
injuries, 37
injury, 37
ink, 16
inlaid, 37
inquire, 40
inquiries, 40
inquiry, 40
insert, 37
inserted, 37
insertion, 37
inside, 37
insist, 37
insisted, 37
inspection, 37
inspiration, 37
install, 37
installation, 37
installed, 37
installment, 37
instance, 52
instant, 52
instead, 37
institute, 40
institution, 40
instruct, 37
instructed, 37
instruction, 37
instructor, 37
instructive, 37
instrument, 37
insurance, 37

118

119

pigs, 18
pin, 6
pink, 16
pins, 18
pipes, 18
Pittsfield, 52
Pittsburgh, 52
place, 2
places, 5
plain, 6,
Plainfield, 52
plan, 6
planned, 21
plans, 18
plant, 21
planted, 21
plate, 6
Plattsburg, 52
pleadings, 49
pleasant, 21
please, 9
pleased, 9
pleasing, 9
pleasure, 18
pledge, 3
plenty, 21
plow, 19
plug, 13
plumbing, 16
plus, 13
pocket, 4
poems, 11
poetry, 11
poets, 11
point, 21
poison, 10
pole, 6
policy, 6
polish, 6
political, 25
politics, 6
pool, 13
poor, 13
popular, 4
population, 50
porch, 6
port, 32
portable, 32
portfolio, 32
portion, 8
ports, 32
position, 47
positive, 26
positively, 26
possession, 8
possibilities, 29
possible, 23
possibly, 9
post, 18
post card, 35
postage, 35
post office, 35
postal, 35
postdate, 35
posted, 20
posthaste, 35
postmark, 35
postmaster, 35
postpaid, 35
postpone, 35
postponed, 35
postscript, 35
pound, 34
pounds, 34
powder, 19
power, 19
powerful, 29
practical, 25
practically, 25
practice, 18
precaution, 8

precedent, 31
predict, 33
prefer, 6
preferred, 17
preliminary, 41
premises, 5
premium, 22
preparation, 8
prepare, 2
prepared, 17
prescription, 8
presence, 34
present, 34
presented, 34
president, 31
presses, 5
pressure, 18
presumably, 50
presume, 50
presumed, 50
presumptive, 50
prettiest, 33
pretty, 6
prevent, 21
prevented, 21
prevention, 8
previous, 22
previously, 22
prices, 5
Princeton, 53
principal, 18
principally, 9
printer, 21
prior, 11
private, 6
privilege, 41
privileged, 41
privileges, 41
probable, 34
probably, 34
probate, 23
problem, 23
procedure, 23
proceed, 23
proceedings, 49
process, 23
processes, 23
procure, 18
produce, 22
produced, 22
producers, 22
produces, 22
product, 33
production, 13
productive, 33
professional, 23
professor, 23
profit, 23
profitable, 23
profitably, 23
program, 29
progress, 26
progressive, 26
prohibit, 23
project, 33
prominence, 20
prominent, 21
promise, 23
promised, 23
promises, 23
promote, 23
promotion, 23
prompt, 21
promptly, 21
promptness, 21
proof, 23
proper, 23
properly, 23
property, 26
proportion, 23
proportionate, 23
proposal, 47

proposed, 47
proposes, 47
proposition, 47
propositions, 47
proprietor, 23
propriety, 40
prosecute, 52
prosecution, 52
prospect, 33
prospective, 33
prosperity, 29
prosperous, 23
protect, 33
protected, 33
protection, 8
protest, 33
protested, 33
proud, 19
prove, 23
proved, 23
proven, 23
provide, 23
provided, 23
provision, 23
prune, 13
psychological, 40
psychology, 40
public, 45
publication, 45
publications, 45
publish, 45
published, 45
publishers, 45
pull, 13
pulled, 17
pump, 16
punch, 16
purchase, 32
purchased, 32
purchases, 32
purchasing, 32
pure, 19
purloin, 23
purple, 23
purpose, 26
purposes, 26
pursuant, 23
pursue, 23
pursued, 23
pursuit, 23
push, 13
put, 4
qualifications, 29
qualities, 29
quantities, 45
quantity, 45
quart, 32
quarter, 32
quarterly, 32
queen, 15
query, 15
question, 49
questions, 49
quick, 15
quicker, 15
quickest, 33
quiet, 15
quit, 15
quite, 15
quota, 15
quotation, 41
quote, 15
quoted, 20
radiation, 11
radiator, 11
radical, 25
radio, 11
radius, 22
rag, 6
railroad, 51
railroads, 51
railway, 15

raise, 18
ran, 6
random, 31
range, 2
rapid, 6
rapidly, 9
rarely, 9
rate, 1
rated, 20
rates, 18
rather, 14
ratification, 29
ratify, 29
ration, 8
raw, 4
reach, 6
reached, 2
reaches, 18
read, 6
reader, 1
readers, 2
readily, 9
ready, 6
real, 1
realize, 18
reappear, 12
reason, 10
reasonable, 23
reasonably, 10
reasons, 12
rebate, 12
recent, 21
recall, 6
receipt, 12
receive, 12
reception, 12
rechecked, 12
reciprocate, 39
recitation, 41
reclaim, 12
recline, 12
recognize, 51
recognized, 51
recommend, 34
recommendation, 41
recommended, 34
reconcile, 37
reconstruction, 37
record, 17
redemption, 31
reduce, 22
reduced, 22
reduces, 22
reduction, 13
refer, 51,
reference, 51
referred, 51
referring, 51
refers, 51
refining, 12
reflect, 33
reflected, 33
refund, 21
refusal, 39
refused, 39
refuses, 39
regain, 12
regard, 49
regards, 49
region, 10
register, 10
registered, 17
regret, 6
regular, 45
regularly, 45
reimburse, 37
reimbursed, 37
reimbursement, 37
rejected, 33
related, 20
relation, 8
relationship, 25

121

122

123

Printed in the United States
106856LV00002B/247/A